Sweet Dreams Stories

Contents

No One Like You

Ruff was hungry. A **huge** grumble rumbled round his tummy. He could hear Rufus clattering round in the kitchen. A delicious smell of freshly baked cakes sailed past his nose.

"Yummy," thought Ruff.

Ruff skipped into the kitchen – Rufus was tidying up. "Would you like some help?" asked Ruff. "I could try one of those cakes for you."

"Oh, really!" said Rufus, smiling.

"No one makes cakes like you," said Ruff.

Ruff was bored. He twiddled his fingers, tapped his toes and twiddled his fingers again. He had no one to play with.

Later, Ruff tip-toed back into the living room – Rufus was reading.
"Would you like something better to read?" asked Ruff. "I could find you an exciting story."
"Oh, really!" said Rufus, smiling.

"No one tells a story like you," said Ruff.

Ruff was fed up. He was trying to make a model car. He fiddled and twiddled and fiddled, but he couldn't put it together.

Then he had an idea!

Ruff galloped into the garden–Rufus was digging.

"Would you like something fun to do?" asked Ruff. "I could let you help me with my model car."

"Oh, really!" said Rufus, smiling.

"No one's as much fun as you,"
said Ruff.

It was bedtime! Rufus tucked Ruff into bed. Ruff was feeling scared. He didn't like the shadows that flickered all round – it was very quiet.

Then he had an idea!

Ruff crept out of his bedroom and into Rufus' room.

Rufus was snoring loudly. It made Ruff giggle and wake Rufus up.

"Would you like someone to cuddle?" asked Ruff. "I'm very good at cuddling."

"Oh, really!" said Rufus, smiling.

"No one cuddles like you,"

yawned Ruff, climbing into
Rufus' bed.

"Oh, really!" said Rufus...

"Well, no one loves you as much as I do, because there's no one like you."

If You Hold My Hand

Oakey's mum opened the front door. "Come on, Oakey. Let's go outside and explore."

But Oakey wasn't really sure. He was only small, and the world looked big and scary.

"Only if you promise to
hold my hand," said Oakey.

So Oakey's mum led him down the long lane.
Oakey wished he was back at home again!

"This looks like a great place to play.
Shall we take a look? What do you say?"
asked Oakey's mum.

"Only if you hold my hand," said Oakey.

And Oakey did it!

"Look at me! I can do it!" he cried.

"This slide looks fun. Would you like to try?" asked Oakey's mum.

Oakey looked at the ladder. It **stretched** right up to the sky.

“I’m only small,” said Oakey. “I don’t know if I can climb that high – *unless you hold my hand.*”

And Oakey did it

"Wheee! Did you see me?" he cried.

"We'll take
a short cut
through the
wood," said
Oakey's mum.

"I'm not sure if we should," said Oakey.
"It looks dark in there. Well, I suppose we could – *will you hold my hand?*"

And Oakey did it!

"Boo! I scared you!" he cried.

Deep in the wood Oakey found a stream, shaded by beautiful tall trees.

"Stepping stones, look!" said Oakey's mum. "Do you think you could jump across these?"

"Maybe," said Oakey. "*I just need you to hold my hand, please.*"

And Oakey did it!

One...

two...

three...

four...

"Your turn now, Mum," cried Oakey, holding out his hand.

Beyond the wood, Oakey and his mum ran up the hill, and all the way down to the sea.

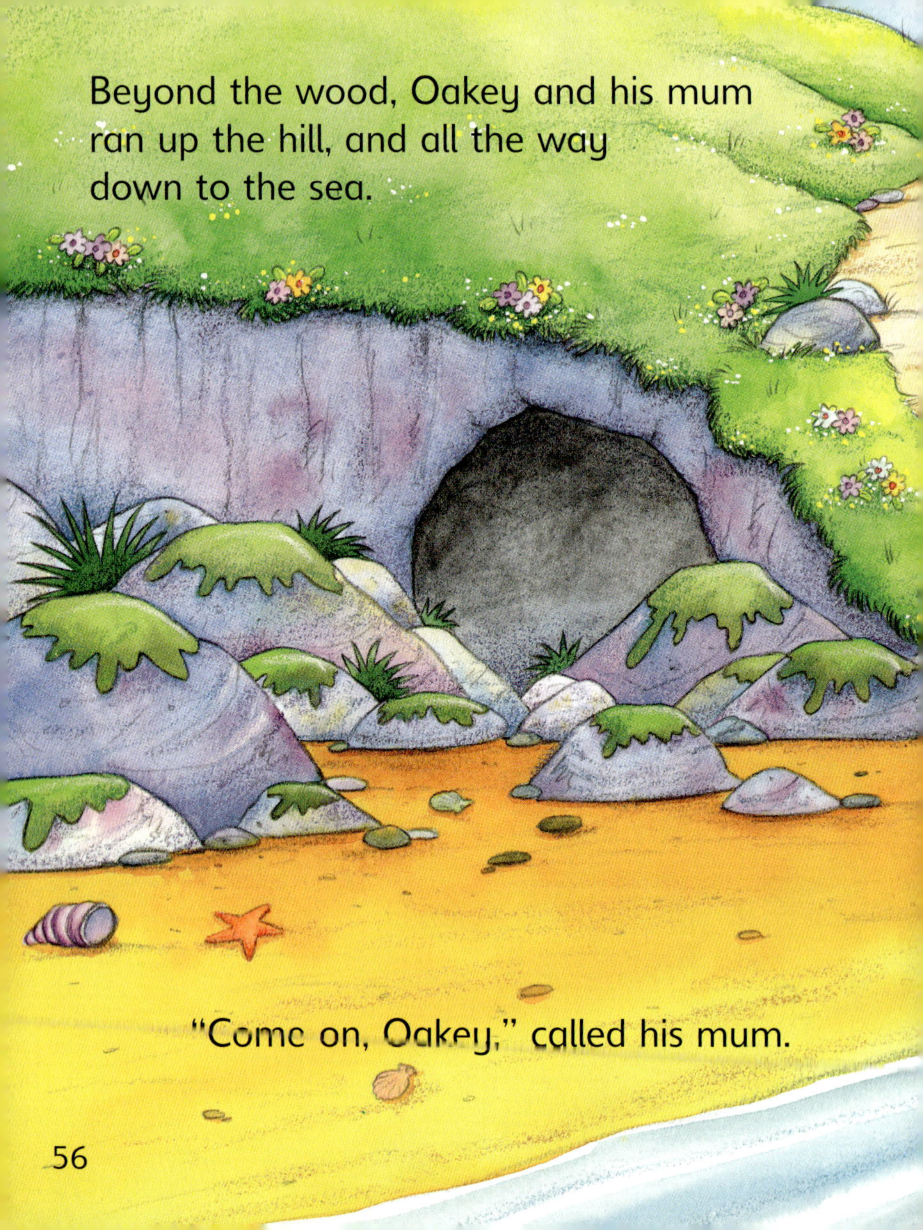

"Come on, Oakey," called his mum.

"Would you like to paddle in the sea with me?"

But the sea looked big, and he was only small.

Suddenly, Oakey knew that didn't matter at all. He turned to his mum and smiled...

"I can do **anything** if you hold my hand," he said.

Just as Well, Really!

Rumpus liked water.

He liked the
drippinginess and
droppiness,

the splashiness
and sloppiness
of it!

He liked it so much that, whenever there
was water around...

...Rumpus somehow always managed to–

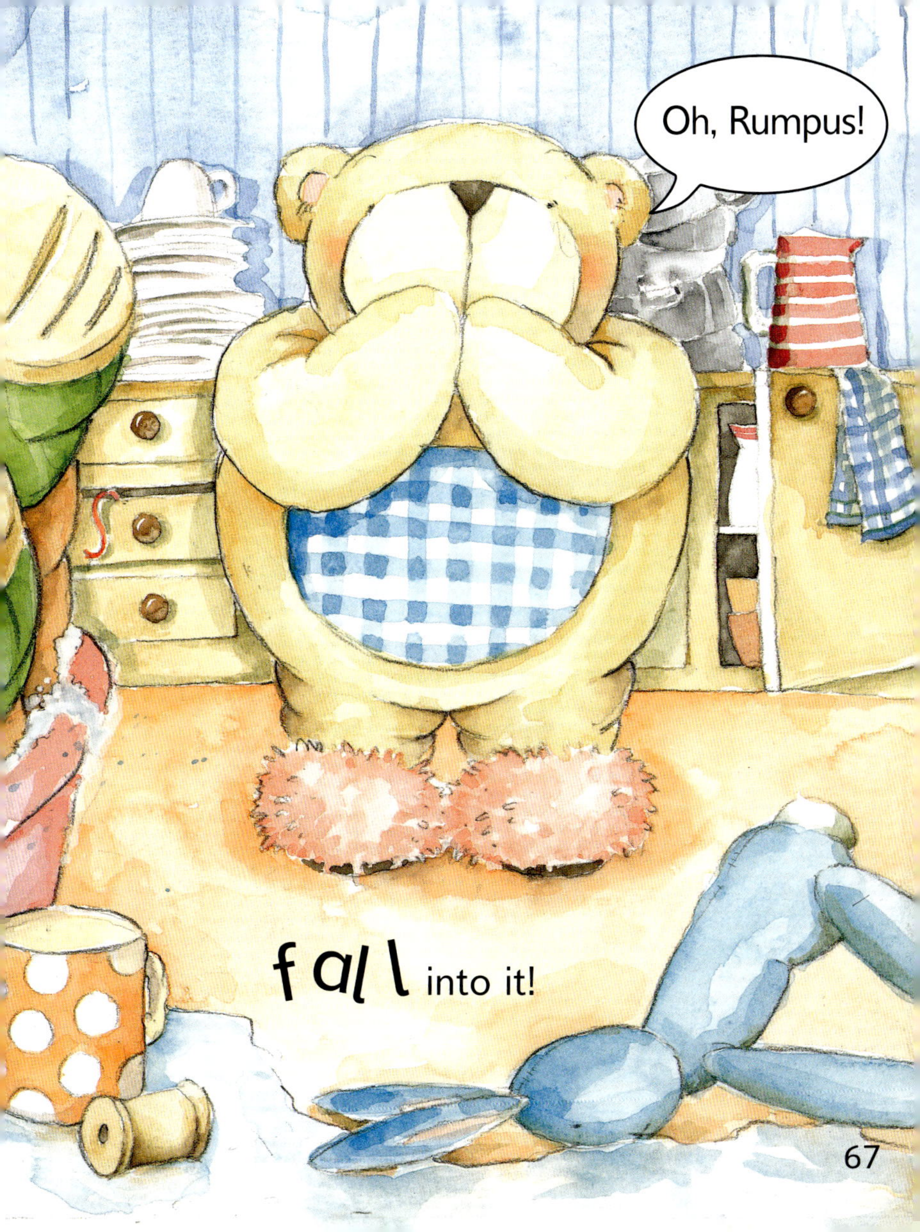

fall into it!

But Mum loved Rumpus, so

very time, she simply sighed—and she mopped up the mess.

Rumpus loved mud.

He loved the way you could

plodge

in it,

splodge

in it,

slide

in it, and

glide

in it!

He loved it so much that, whenever
there was mud around...

...Rumpus somehow always managed to–

get covered in it!

Pop

But Dad loved Rumpus, so

every time, he simply sighed–and he sponged off the splatters.

Rumpus enjoyed paint.

He liked to
splatter
and
dash it,

to spread
and
splash
it!

He enjoyed it so much that,
whenever there was paint
around...

...Rumpus somehow managed to– get it everywhere!

But Rumpus' brother loved him, so

every time, he simply sighed—and cleaned himself up.

Rumpus liked to find out how things worked.

He loved the prodding and probing,

the wiggling and the jiggling, the unscrewing and the undoing!

e loved it so much that, whenever Rumpus was around...

...things didn't work for long!

Oh, Rumpus!

But Granny loved Rumpus,
so she simply sighed – and
she tidied away the clutter.

Rumpus loved his
mum, dad...

brother and granny...

Rumpus' mum, dad, brother and granny loved Rumpus...

...just as well, really!

On my Own

Deep in the jungle, where only wild things go, Mungo's mum was teaching him what a young monkey needs to know. "Some things just aren't safe to try alone," she said.

"Why not?" said Mungo. "I'm big enough to do things–

on my own!"

“Now Mungo,”

said Mum, “listen carefully, please. We’re going to go through these trees. Stay close to me, and hold my hand. Did you hear what I said?

Do you understand?”

"It's okay, Mum. I won't slip or fall. I can swing across there with no trouble at all," said Mungo. "I'm big enough to do it–

on my own!" And off he swung!

"Hissss,"
hissed Snake,
in a snake sort
of wail.

"That pesky Mungo
pulled my tail!"

And did Mungo hear poor old Snake groan?

No!

Mungo just laughed.
"I told you I could do it
on my own."

"Now, we're going to cross the river using these stones," said Mum. "But, Mungo, I'd rather you didn't do this alone."

"But Mum," said Mungo, and he ran on without stopping, "I'm really good at jumping and hopping. I'm big enough to do it–

on my own!"

And off he sprang!

"That Mungo trampled on my nose!" said Croc.

"Next time, I'll nibble off his toes!"

And did Mungo hear poor old Croc groan?

No! Mungo just smiled. "I told you I could do it

on my own."

"Mungo," said Mum, with a serious look on her face, "the jungle can be a dangerous place. There are all sorts of corners for creatures to hide, so, from here on, make sure that you stay by my side."

"Oh, Mum," said Mungo, "I don't need to wait for you. I can easily find my own way through. I'm big enough to do it–
on my own!"

Lion rubbed the lump on his nose.

"Ouch!

That Mungo's so careless!" he said.

And did Mungo hear poor old Lion groan?

No! Mungo just grinned. "I told you I could do it **on my own.**"

"I think I've had quite enough for one day,"
Mum said. "So off you go, little monkey!

Now it really is time for bed!"

It was Mungo's turn to let out a groan.
"I don't want to go to bed–
on my own!"
"Don't worry," said Mum. "Come on,
kiss me goodnight, and I promise I'll
hold you and cuddle you tight."

Lion roared, "Is that Mungo still awake?"
"Yes!" snapped Crocodile.

"Lets help him go to sleep," hissed Snake.

And into the velvety, starry sky drifted the sounds of a jungle lullaby.

Guess What I Want?

"Guess what I want?" said Ruff to Rufus.

"Something from me?" asked Rufus.
"Now, let me see – what could it be?"

"You've got to guess,"
said Ruff.

"You want me to tie a string to the moon, so you can pull it around like a giant balloon?" said Rufus.

"We could tie the moon
to the post of your bed,
to shine through the night
above your head."

"Would you really get me the moon?" asked Ruff.

"Well, it would be quite hard to climb up that high, but for you, of course, I'd give it a try," said Rufus.

"Guess again," laughed Ruff.

"You want me to catch you
a shining white star,
and capture its bright light
for you in a jar?"
said Rufus.

"It would twinkle all night and light up your dreams,

and dance round your room, mixed with yellow moonbeams."

P.Venus.

"Would you really fetch
me a star?" asked Ruff.

"Well, catching a star isn't easy to do,
but I'd give it a try,
because I love you," said Rufus.

"Guess again,"
laughed Ruff.

"You want me to capture the song of the breeze,
as it lulls its way gently through leaves on the trees?
said Rufus.

"You'd be able to turn on the breeze's soft tune,
for the starlight to dance along with the moon."

P.Venus.

“Would you really bring me the song of the breeze?” asked Ruff.

“Well, the breeze moves so fast, it isn’t easy to do, but I’d find a way to do it for you,” said Rufus.

Ruff thought hard.

"To tie down the moon, wouldn't be right. And the sky is the place to leave the starlight. It wouldn't be fair to stop the wind's song. Now, try one more guess – your first three were wrong!"

"I know. I was teasing.
I think you want this..."

...a huge great big cuddle,
nd a lovely big kiss!"

A Goodnight Kiss

"It's bedtime now,
Oakey," said Mum.

Oakey curled up in the chair.
His ears began to droop and he muttered,
"Oh, that's not fair!"

"Have a drink first," smiled Mum, "then you must go."

Five minutes more!" begged Oakey.

Mum answered, **"No!"**

Oakey's ears drooped and off he went.
But he was **back in a flash!**

"Where's your drink?" asked Mum.
"You haven't been very long.
You look scared, Oakey.
Is there something wrong?"

"There's a monster

in the kitchen,
with long, white shaggy hair,
lurking in the corner,
behind the rocking chair,"
said Oakey.

Mum laughed.
"Oh, Oakey, you've made a mistake.
That's no monster. It's a mop." And she gave the mop a shake.

Oakey's ears drooped
and off he went.
But he was
back in a flash!

"What's the matter?"
asked Mum.

"There's a ghost
in the hallway, hovering around.
Look, there it is floating
just above the ground,"
he wailed.

"Oh, Oakey, you've made a mistake.
That's no ghost.
It's just an old coat, hanging on
the hook.
Coats don't float!" laughed Mum.

Oakey's ears drooped and
off he went.
But he was
back in a flash!

"Why aren't you in bed, Oakey?"
asked Mum.

"There's a great big lump

beneath the sheets.
It's waiting to get me.
I'm scared it's going
to pounce. Please come
and see," sniffed Oakey.

"Oh, Oakey, you've made a mistake.
The only thing underneath the sheets,
is your old teddy bear," smiled Mum.

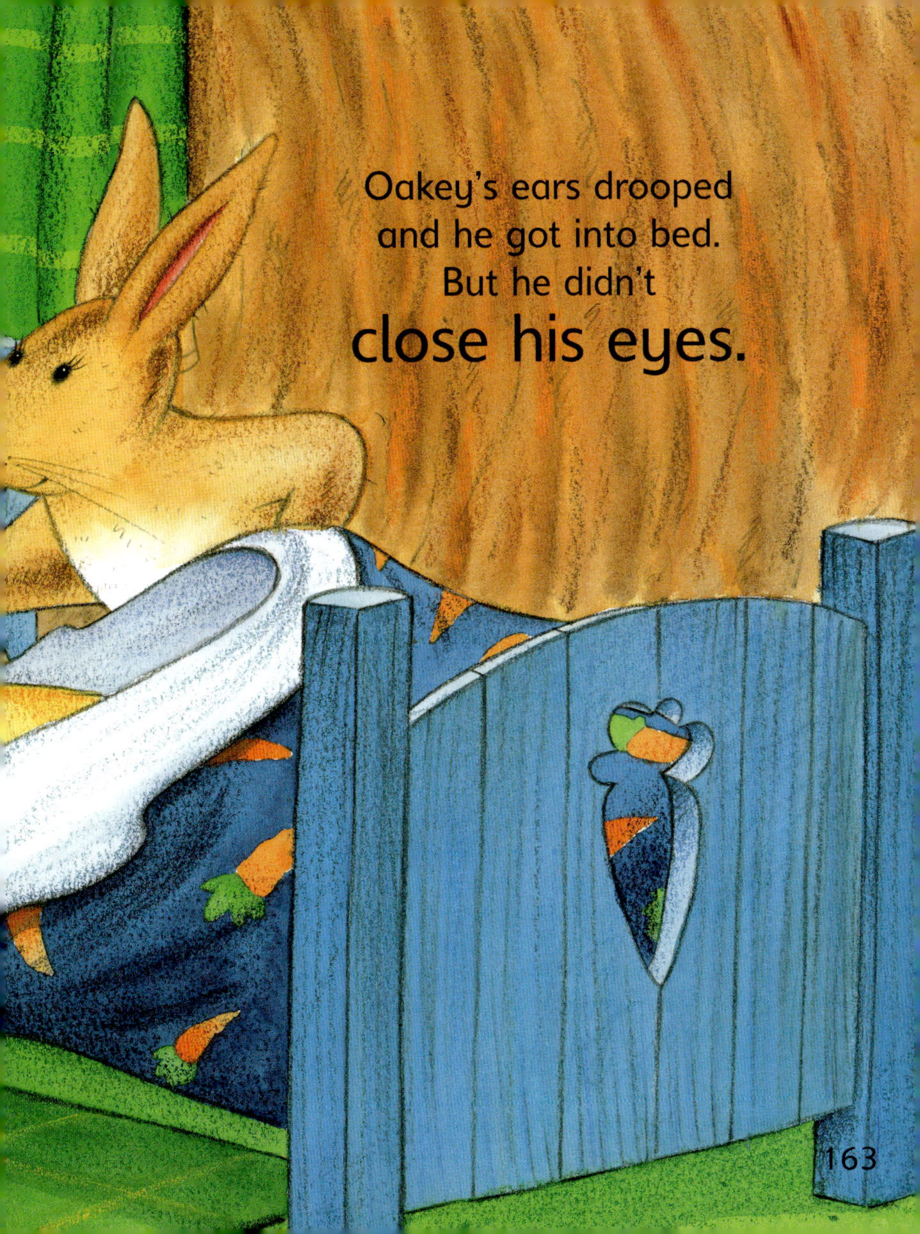

Oakey's ears drooped
and he got into bed.
But he didn't
close his eyes.

"Why aren't you asleep?"
asked Mum.

"There are
huge creepy crawlies
underneath my bed.
And I can't get the thought of them
out of my head,"
complained Oakey.

"They're just your slippers, Oakey, so there's no need to hide. They be won't creeping anywhere without your feet inside," grinned Mum.

"That's it now, Oakey. Time to say goodnight."

Mum turned and left the room, switching off the light.

And then Oakey saw it,
standing by the door.

The monster!

It moved across the floor and walked straight towards him, with its arms stretched out. Oakey's mouth opened, but he found he couldn't shout.

The monster leaned over him and Oakey closed his eyes. What happened next gave Oakey an enormous surprise. The monster picked him up and cuddled him tight. Monsters just don't do that.

This couldn't be right!

Then Mum's voice whispered,
"Don't worry, it's just me.
When I said 'Goodnight' just now,
I forgot to give you this."

Then 'Monster Mum' gave Oakey
a goodnight kiss!

Kiss it Better

Rumpus was romping around the living room. He cartwheeled across the carpet.

He turned a somersault on the sofa.

"Be careful!" called Mum.

Too late! Rumpus slipped from the sofa, crumpled onto the carpet and banged his head on the floor.

"My head hurts!"

he groaned.

"Come here and I'll **kiss it better,"** said Mum.

She hugged Rumpus and planted a kiss on his forehead.

"Now, go and find something less rowdy to do," she said.

Rumpus rushed out into the garden
and began to ride his bike.
Round and round he raced.

"Watch out!"
called Mum.

5

Too late!

Rumpus crashed into the corner of the wheelbarrow...

and tumbled to the ground and grazed his knee.

"My leg hurts!"

he wailed.

"Come here and I'll kiss it better," said Mum.

She hugged Rumpus and planted a kiss on his knee.

“Now, go and find something safer to do,” she said.

Rumpus ran up the grassy slope.

Then he rolled down.

"Roly poly, down the hill," he sang.

"Look where you're going!"

called Mum.

Too late!

Rumpus rolled right into
the rose bush.
The thorns scratched him all
along his arm.

"My arm's sore!"
cried Rumpus.

"Come here and I'll **kiss it better,"** said Mum and she planted kisses all up his arm.

"Now, try and
keep out of
trouble,"
she said.

Mum went into the kitchen.
"I need a break,"
she thought.

She made a cup of tea.
She cut herself a slice of cake.
Then, she sat down for five minutes.

Just as she picked up her cup,
Rumpus zoomed into the kitchen...

on his **skateboard.**

“Rumpus!”said Mum.
“Can’t you find something more sensible to do?”

Mum moved into the living room.
"I need a rest," she thought.
She sat down on the sofa and picked up the paper.

"Boom!
Boom!
Boom!"

In marched Rumpus,
banging on his drum.
Mum sighed a loud sigh.

"Is anything wrong?" asked Rumpus.

"I've got a headache!" said Mum.

"Never mind," smiled Rumpus, throwing his arms round her. "I'll soon kiss *it* better."

Lost and Alone

Deep in the jungle, Mungo was trying to slip off through the trees.
"Mungo, tell me where you're going, please," called Mum.
"What are you planning to do today?"

“I’m just going to play,” smiled
Mungo.
“Okay,” said Mum.
“But no monkey business!”

Elephant was enjoying a peaceful drink, when Mungo crept up and yelled, "Hi, Elephant!

Want to play?"

Then he added, "I know a good game."

"Oh, yes?" said Elephant, suspiciously. "What's its name?"

"Funny faces!"said Mungo.

"What do you say?"

"I'm not sure," said Elephant.

"I don't know how to play."

"Easy" said Mungo. "All you have to do, is pull a funny face. Look, I'll show you."

And he took hold of Elephant's trunk.

Mungo wound Elephant's trunk round and round and slipped the end through.
He pulled it into a knot.

"Wow, Elephant!" he giggled.

"What a funny face you've got!"

"Hey!" gurgled Elephant. "How do I get out of this?"

But Mungo was gone!

Down by the river bank,
Crocodile was trying to nap,
when Mungo jumped out of the trees,
and gave his nose a tap.

"Want to play?" Mungo asked.
"I know a good game."

"Really?" said Crocodile,
suspiciously.
"What's its name?"

"Funny Faces," said Mungo.

"What do you say?"

"I'm not sure," said Crocodile.
"I don't know how to play."

"Easy," said Mungo. "All you have to do, is pull a funny face. Look, I'll show you." And he took hold of Crocodile's jaws.

Mungo pulled on one jaw, and pushed on the other.
Then he jammed them both together.

"Hey, Croc!" he giggled.

"That's a really funny face!"

"Help!" choked Crocodile.

"How do I get out of this?"

But Mungo was gone!

Lion was trying to have a laze in the sun, when Mungo swung down and asked, "Want some fun?" Then he added, "Come on. I know a good game."

"Yeah?" said Lion, suspiciously. "What's its name?"

"Funny Faces,"
said Mungo.

"What do you say?"

"I'm not sure," said Lion.
"I don't know how to play."

"Easy," said Mungo.
"All you have to do, is pull a
funny face. Look, I'll show you."

And he took hold of
Lion's bottom lip.

Mungo pulled the lip up over Lion's nose.
"You see," he said, "that's the way it goes."

Then he ran off, smiling, through the trees.
"Forget what Mum said," thought Mungo.
"I'll do as I please."
He swung through the branches, but, after a while,
Mungo's face lost its smile.
"I don't know where I am!" he wailed.

“That’s a funny face,” said Elephant.
“He wins the game for sure.”
“You’re right,” laughed Lion.
“Come on, Mungo, give us more.”

"It's not a game," howled Mungo.
"I'm lost and alone.
I want my mum! How do I get out of here?
This isn't any fun!"

"Well, shall we help him?" Lion roared.
"What do you think?"

"I'm not sure," said Elephant.
"He did disturb my drink."

"And he woke me up," Crocodile complained,
"which really wasn't fun."

"He wrecked my rest, too," Lion said.
"You're not the only one."

"If we agree to help, Mungo,"
the animals all said. "Then no more funny faces.
Can you get that into your head?"

Mungo looked much happier than he'd
done in quite a while.
"No more tricks!" Mungo promised,
and he thanked each of the three.
"Being lost and alone
wasn't any fun for me!"

This is a Parragon Book
This edition published in 2004

Parragon
Queen Street House
4 Queen Street
Bath, BA1 1HE, UK

Created by The Complete Works
Written by Jillian Harker
Illustrated by Andy Everitt-Stewart,
Louise Gardner, Julie Nicholson and Pamela Venus

ISBN 1-40542-644-6

Printed in China